WILD HORSES

by George Edward Stanley
illustrated by Michael Langham Rowe

To Uncle Hubbard, for giving me my first horse,
and to my family, for all their love and support
G.E.S.

For Sue, Steven, and Julie
and all at Wildlife Art Ltd.
M.L.R.

Special thanks to
Dr. Patrick Thomas, Mammal Department, the Bronx Zoo.

Library of Congress Cataloging-in-Publication Data
Stanley, George Edward.
Wild horses / by George Edward Stanley ; illustrated by Michael Langham Rowe.
    p.   cm. — (Road to reading. Mile 4)
Summary: Discusses the different wild horses that can be found around the
world today, including Chincoteague ponies, Australian brumbies, American
mustangs, and the wild horses of Asia.
ISBN 0-307-26409-2 (pbk.) — ISBN 0-307-46409-1 (GB)
1. Wild horses—Juvenile literature. [1. Wild horses. 2. Horses.] I. Rowe,
Michael Langham, ill. II. Title. III. Series.

SF360 .S72 2001
599.665'5—dc21   00-039341

A GOLDEN BOOK • New York
Golden Books Publishing Company, Inc. New York, New York 10106

ISBN: 0-307-26409-2 (pbk)
ISBN: 0-307-46409-1 (GB)

10 9 8 7 6 5 4 3 2

Contents

Wild Horses of the Past

Scritch! Scratch! Scritch!

A caveman makes marks on a rock wall with a burnt stick. He is drawing a picture—a picture of an animal he saw. The caveman looks at what he's done. He frowns. He adds more marks. Scritch! Scratch! Scritch! Scratch!

He steps back and looks again. Now

it looks like the animal!

The caveman didn't know the name of what he had drawn. But fifteen thousand years later, French hikers found the cave. They knew what the animal was. The caveman had drawn a wild horse!

Long before people walked the earth, horses roamed here. But they didn't look the same as they do now. During the time of dinosaurs, horses looked like small dogs. Over millions of years, horses changed. Their legs got longer. Their heads got bigger. Their toes grew together into hooves.

Six million years ago, horses finally reached the size of most horses today. Back then, all horses were wild. But in time, people came along. At first, they probably hunted horses. Maybe they ate them for food. Maybe they made clothing from horse skin. After a while, people started to look at horses in a different way. Horses seemed smart. They could help.

The people in Asia were the first ones to tame horses. They used horses to pull chariots. The chariots carried soldiers into battle. Later on, people

put saddles and bridles on horses. They rode horses where chariots couldn't go.

Soon, people in other parts of the world picked up the idea. They started taming horses. They started breeding them, too. These horses weren't wild. They were raised to carry people.

But there were still wild horses all over the world. They never pulled a wagon. They never wore a saddle or a bridle. They never even felt the touch of a human being.

This is the story of those wild horses.

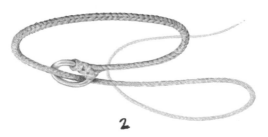

2

Wild Horses of France

The marshes in the south of France are not an easy place to live. During summer, the sun bakes the earth until it cracks. During winter, a thin sheet of icy water covers the land. But in this harsh setting live the Camargue (kah-MARG). The Camargue are the wild white horses of France.

A Camargue's coat is white and silky. It looks like sea foam. This horse may be beautiful, but it's hardy, too. It eats mainly salt grasses and reeds. Most Camargue are still wild. But some are ridden by French cowboys.

French cowboys? Yes. These cowboys take care of the black cattle that live in this part of France.

French cowboys are called *gardiens* (gar-dee-YENZ). They use horsehair ropes and large three-pronged forks to keep the cattle in order.

Back in the 1800s, France owned Louisiana. *Gardiens* came to Louisiana

to watch over the cattle. After Louisiana became part of the United States, some *gardiens* headed west. They used their skills to capture and tame the wild horses there.

Most people think of cowboys as American. But in a way, the first cowboys were actually French!

3
Wild Horses of the Islands

An island may seem like a funny place to find wild horses. After all, how does a horse get on an island? No one knows for sure. Some horses may have swum to islands from wrecked ships. Other horses may have been left behind by early explorers.

We do know how horses got to

Assateague Island. They were
stranded there. This island was once
linked to the mainland by skinny strips
of land. Then, in 1933, a fierce storm
washed away the land. Assateague
turned into an island.

Today, Assateague and its neighbor
island, Chincoteague, are home to

about two hundred horses. Most of them live on Assateague. Assateague is now a national park.

For many years, the horses lived without any help from people. But they weren't very healthy. They drank salt water from the ocean. Sometimes they even ate poison ivy.

Things got worse for the horses in 1943. Part of Assateague was fenced off for wild birds. The horses lost a lot of the land where they grazed. They had to stay in only one section of the island. It was small. It was marshy. Thousands of biting insects bothered

them all summer. And the horses had
no way to get to the sea.

In 1947, Marguerite Henry wrote a
book called *Misty of Chincoteague*. It
was about two kids who earn money
to buy Phantom, the wildest mare on

Assateague Island, and her colt, Misty.

The book was a big success. Until then, hardly anyone outside Virginia knew about these wild horses. In 1961, a movie was made of the book. Soon, people all over America sent money to help the wild horses.

In 1962, there was another big storm. Because the horses were trapped on a small part of the island, many drowned. All the people who fell in love with the horses from the *Misty* book got angry. After that, the horses were no longer fenced off. The most famous wild horses in the world could run free again.

But the islands are not very big. They can support only a couple of hundred horses. So each July, the Chincoteague Fire Department has the horses swim from Assateague to Chincoteague.

Some of the extra foals and
yearlings are sold to happy owners.
The ponies can be trained for kids to
ride. And the money from the sales
helps take care of the rest of the
herds.

4
Wild Horses of the Mountains

Wild horses have lived in the mountains between Spain and France for thousands of years. In winter, the mountains are covered with snow and ice. The temperature drops below freezing for long periods of time. How can a horse live in such a place?

The wild mountain horses have a

thick winter coat. They have a heavy mane and tail to protect them from the cold. It's no problem for them to climb the steep mountain trails—even when the trails are covered with ice and snow.

Mountain horses love cold weather, but they can't stand it when it's hot. During summer, they spend most of their time huddled in the shade of the thick pine forests.

Sometimes, mountain horses are captured and used to smuggle guns and drugs across the mountains. If the smugglers are caught by the police, they're sent to prison. But the horses are set free to roam wild in the mountains again.

5
Wild Horses of the Misty Moors

The Exmoor is the only wild horse left in Great Britain. It lives mainly in a national park. The Exmoor has changed very little over time. Several years ago, the bones of a two-million-year-old horse were found in Alaska. Scientists compared them to an Exmoor skeleton. They were almost the same!

The Exmoor looks different from many horses today. It has a bigger head than other horses. And the Exmoor has hooded eyes. The hoods protect its eyes from wind, rain, and snow.

The moors in Great Britain are like the prairies in America. They have miles and miles of tall grass. The moors get a lot of rain. In winter, it can be extremely cold, and there is always a lot of snow. But this doesn't bother the Exmoor. Its nostrils are

longer than other horses'. The cold air the Exmoor breathes is warmed before it gets to the lungs.

If the Exmoors feel threatened, all the adult horses make a circle around the foals to keep them safe. The herd stallion defends the herd. It lashes out

with its teeth. It slashes at the enemies with its front hooves. But there are some enemies the Exmoor can't fight.

The future of the Exmoor in Great Britain is not very bright. Scientists think it's hard for them to breed away from the moors. The land where these horses live is being used for houses and business centers. Soon, without its moors, the Exmoor may become extinct.

6

Wild Horses of Mongolia

In 1879, a colonel in the Imperial Russian Army went to Mongolia. His job was to make a map of the area for the Russian government. He set up camp at the edge of the Gobi Desert. Nearby was a mountain range that the local people called the Mountains of the Yellow Horses.

Early one morning, the colonel heard the thunder of pounding hooves. The sound was coming from the mountains. He ran out of his tent to see what it was.

In a few minutes, the colonel saw hundreds of horses racing across the desert sand. They looked like yellow zebras. But they weren't zebras. They

were Mongolian wild horses. No one outside of Mongolia had ever seen these horses!

The colonel was very excited. With help from some of the local people, the colonel caught several of the horses. He took them back to Russia. They were let out on a large estate. People from all over Russia came to see them. They fell in love with the funny-looking yellow horses.

While the Russians adored the horses, the people in Mongolia kept hunting the Mongolian wild horse for its meat and its skin. Soon, a zoo was almost the only place to see the horses. The zoos kept the Mongolian wild horse from becoming extinct.

In the past few years, some horses have been set free on the land where they used to live. They are having babies, new horses born wild. Maybe someday the "yellow zebras" will thunder across their old mountains again.

7

Wild Horses of the Outback

Before 1788, Australia had no horses. But then people from England and South Africa settled there. They brought their horses with them.

In 1851, gold was discovered in the outback of Australia. Many miners used horses to carry their food and equipment. But some of these horses

strayed from the mining towns. They ran wild in the rough scrub country. The Australians called these horses brumbies.

The brumbies ate the grass that Australian farmers needed for their cattle. That made the farmers mad. They shot the brumbies for sport.

By the 1960s, there were so many brumbies the Australian government decided to get rid of them. Hunters started shooting them from airplanes. In just one month, over seventeen thousand brumbies were killed.

People all over the world got angry

about this. The shootings stopped. Now, the tough and wary brumbies once again live in the outback in large numbers.

But many people in Australia don't like the brumbies. Brumbies can't really be used for anything. Some people are still trying to find ways to get rid of some of them.

8
Wild Horses of the American West

Imagine the Wild West. What do you think of? Pioneers? Cowboys? Wild horses?

The wild horses of the West are called mustangs. Mustang comes from the Spanish word *mesteño*. *Mesteño* means a horse that has escaped or strayed from the range and become wild. In the 1500s, Spanish conquerors brought horses to America. Some ran away from their owners. They became the mustangs.

At first, Native Americans feared the Spanish horses. They thought mustangs were gods with strong powers. Then the Spanish men went away. The horses were left behind. That's when Native Americans started riding them. The horses made hunting easier. A fine horse even became a sign of wealth.

A few years later, French *gardiens* headed west from Louisiana. They were followed by woodsmen from Kentucky,

Tennessee, and North Carolina. And finally, Mexican herdsmen came up north from Mexico. They all met on the great plains and became American cowboys. They used mustangs to herd cattle to market.

By the middle of the 1800s, there were over three million mustangs in the West. But before long, the Wild West wasn't so wild anymore. The gold rush ended. Native Americans moved to reservations. And most cowboys

were seen only in rodeos. The mustangs had their problems, too.

In the 1940s, hunters began killing these horses and turning them into pet food. By 1970, there were fewer than twenty thousand mustangs left. When the American people found out, they were horrified. They made the government stop the hunters.

Now the mustangs are protected. The herds have begun to grow again. You can see them running free in Colorado, Nevada, and Wyoming.

9

Wild Horses—
Today and Tomorrow

A small band of wild horses grazes
peacefully on the slopes of a mountain.
Suddenly, the herd stallion whinnies. It
is time to look for water. The stallion
lifts his head. He flares his nostrils. He
gallops to the rear of the herd and
begins to drive the horses down the
mountain. Dust flies and rocks clatter.

With pounding hooves and snorting breath, the herd rushes toward the sparkling river below.

Fifty years ago, it was hard to find a place where horses ran wild. In Asia, in Australia, and in America, wild horses were in danger.

Hunters killed them for pet food. Farmers and ranchers killed them because they ate the cattle's grass.

But then something wonderful happened. Ordinary people put an end to it. They told their governments that they wanted to save the wild horses.

Why did they care? Why do people love wild horses so much?

Maybe it's because people see themselves in the horses. Wild horses have no masters. No one rides them. No one fences them up at night.

Wild horses are free.